This workbook covers the macro economics topics which are not in the AS specification for each exam board.

As all exam boards are slightly different you may have covered some of these topics or covered them in less detail at AS level

The specification links refer to the A level specification.
- AQA The national and international economy (7136)
- Edexcel Theme 4 A global perspective(9ECO)
- OCR Macroeconomics (H460/02)

Contents

Chapter 1 Globalisation — 4

Chapter 2 Specialisation and Trade — 8

Chapter 3 Trading blocs and Protectionism — 15

Chapter 4 Balance of Payments — 24

Chapter 5 Exchange Rates — 30

Chapter 6 Poverty and Inequality — 37

Chapter 7 Development — 42

Chapter 8 The Financial Sector — 49

Chapter 9 Government Intervention — 53

	AQA	Edexcel	OCR
Chapter 1	4.2.6.1	4.1.1	4.3
Chapter 2	4.2.6.2	4.1.2 4.1.3 4.1.4 4.1.9	4.1 4.3
Chapter 3	4.2.6.2	4.1.5 4.1.6	4.4
Chapter 4	4.2.6.3	4.1.7	2.5
Chapter 5	4.2.6.4	4.1.8	4.2 4.3
Chapter 6	4.1.7.3	4.2.1 4.2.2	2.7
Chapter 7	4.2.6.5	4.3.1 4.3.2 4.3.3	2.2 5.2 5.3
Chapter 8	4.2.4.1 4.2.4.2 4.2.4.3 4.2.4.4	4.4.1 4.4.2 4.4.3	5.1 5.2 5.3
Chapter 9	4.2.4.3 4.2.5.1 4.2.5.2	4.5.1 4.5.2 4.5.3 4.5.4	2.6 2.9 3.1 3.2 3.3

Chapter 1 Globalisation

1. What is globalisation? (1)

The increasing connections between economies and people worldwide

2. What are the three main characteristics of globalisation? (3)

- Increased trade and investment between countries
- Growth of multinational corporations
- Faster communication

3. What is the difference between a developing and emerging country? (2)

- Developing country has a low income economy and weaker infrastructure while an emerging on is ~~rapidly~~ rapidly industrialising and experiencing economic ~~growth~~

4. What is a multinational corporation? Give an example (2)

- A corporation that operates in multiple countries
- Apple

5. What is the difference between outsourcing and offshoring? (2)

Outsourcing is hiring an external company for certain tasks while offshoring is relocating operations to another country for cost savings.

6. Give two reasons why a firm may locate in another country (2)

- To reduce costs
- To access new markets

7. Why does the removal of tariffs lead to more trade? (2)

Removing tariffs lowers costs making imports cheaper and increasing trade

8. Why does an increase in global production standards lead to more trade? (2)

Higher production standards improve product quality and reduce trade barriers, making trade easier

9. Why might a government provide incentives for foreign firms to locate in their country? (2)

Governments attract foreign firms to create jobs and boost investment

10. Give two benefits to consumers of globalisation (2)

- More choice
- Lower prices

11. Give two benefits to producers or globalisation (2)

- Producers access larger markets
- Lower production costs

12. Give two benefits to the government of globalisation (2)

- Gov gains higher tax revenue
- Economic growth

13. Give two benefits to workers of globalisation (2)

- Workers get more job opportunitys
- Workers get skill development

14. Give two problems to the environment of globalisation (2)

- Causes pollution
- Resource depletion

15. Give two problems to consumers of globalisation (2)

- Loss of local businesses
- Exploitation risks

16. Give two problems to producers of globalisation (2)

- They face tougher competition
- Supply chain risks

17. Give two problems to the government of globalisation (2)

- Gov struggles to regulate businesses
- Gov faces economic instability

18. Explain why globalisation can lead to increased inequality (2)

Because it benefits the rich more, increasing inequality

19. Give two problems of globalisation for developing countries (2)

- Potential worker exploitation
- Economic dependance

20. Give two benefits of globalisation for developing countries (2)

Developing countries gain investment and technology

21. Give two problems of globalisation for developed countries (2)

Developed countries face job losses and market dependance

22. Give two benefits of globalisation for developed countries (2)

Developed countries benefit from cheaper production and expand markets

Chapter 2 Specialisation and Trade

1. Give three reasons for international trade (3)

2. Give three advantages of specialisation (3)

3. Give three problems with international trade (3)

4. Give three problems with specialisation (3)

5. Define absolute advantage (2)

6. Define comparative advantage (2)

7. The table below shows maximum output of apples or bananas for two countries

	Units of apples		Units of bananas
Country A	1000.	or	2000
Country B	2000.	or	3000

a) Which country has an absolute advantage in apples? (1)

b) Which country has an absolute advantage in bananas? (1)

c) Which country has a comparative advantage in apples? (1)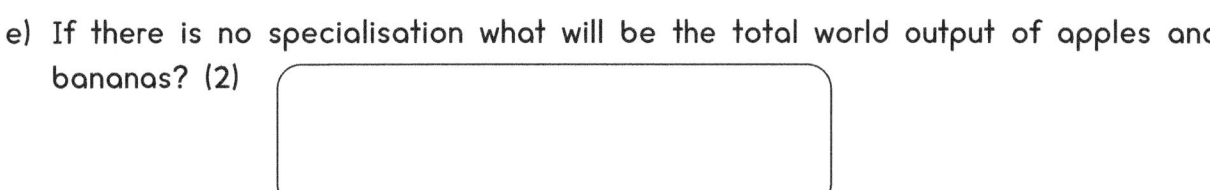

d) Which country has a comparative advantage in bananas (1)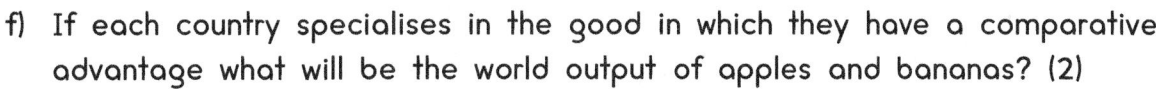

e) If there is no specialisation what will be the total world output of apples and bananas? (2)

f) If each country specialises in the good in which they have a comparative advantage what will be the world output of apples and bananas? (2)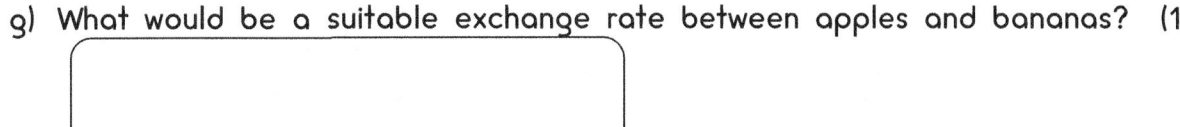

g) What would be a suitable exchange rate between apples and bananas? (1)

8. The table below shows the maximum output of chairs and tables for two countries.

	Units of chairs	Units of tables
Country A	100 or	40
Country B	180 or	60

a) Draw a production possibility curve to illustrate the possible outcomes for each country (3)

b) Which country has an absolute advantage in chairs? (1)

c) Which country has an absolute advantage in tables? (1)

d) Which country has a comparative advantage in chairs? (1)

e) Which country has a comparative advantage in tables? (1)

f) What is the total world output of each good if there is no specialisation? (2)

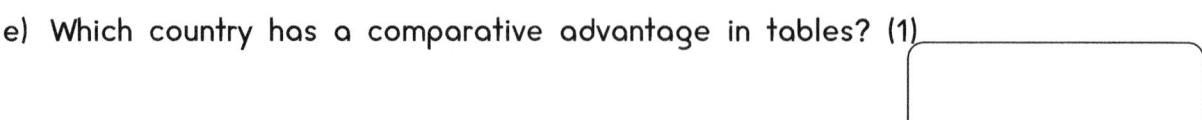

g) If each country specialises in the good in which they have a comparative advantage what will be the total output of each good? (2)

h) What would be a suitable exchange rate between tables and chairs? (1)

9. Give three assumptions which have been made when determining the benefits from specialisation (3)

10. Give the formula for terms of trade (1)

11. What does it mean by an improvement in terms of trade? (1)

12. For each situation state where there will be a worsening, improvement or no change in the terms of trade (5)
a) Import and export prices both increase by the same amount

b) Import prices increase, export prices fall

c) Import prices decrease, export prices increase

d) Import prices rise faster than export prices

e) Import prices rise slower than export prices

13. For each statement below state whether it is most likely true for developed, developing or both. (3)

a) They have a comparative advantage in primary goods

b) They have a comparative advantage in technology

c) They do most of their trade with developed countries

13. Name two emerging economies which are now important global traders (2)

14. Which country do the largest proportion of UK exports go? (1)

15. Where do the largest proportion of UK imports come from? (2)

16. State three ways in which the pattern of trade has changed for the UK in the last 20 years (3)

17. What does it mean if a country has become more internationally competitive? (2)

18. Give three non-price factors which are used to determine competitiveness (3)

19. Explain why an increase in the value of a currency makes a country less internationally competitive (2)

20. Explain how relative unit labour costs contribute to competitive (2)

21. Explain three policies the government could use to improve a countries international competitiveness (6)

22. Explain the impact on the macro economic indicators of reduced international competitiveness (6)

Chapter 3 Trading Blocs and Protectionsism

1. What is the meaning of free trade? (2)

2. What is the purpose of the WTO? (1)

3. What is the meaning of protectionism? (1)

4. Explain four reasons why governments might want to use protectionist measures (8)

5. Explain four problems with protectionism (8)

6. Define tariff (2)

7. What is the purpose of a tariff? (2)

8. Draw a diagram showing the imposition of a tariff (4)

9. Use your diagram to identify the following areas (12)
a) Original domestic demand
b) New domestic demand
c) Original consumer surplus
d) New consumer surplus
e) Original domestic supply

f) New domestic supply

g) Original level of imports

h) New level of imports

i) Original producer surplus

j) New producer surplus

k) Tax revenue received by the government

l) Net welfare loss

10. Explain three problems with imposing tariffs (6)

11. Define quota (1)

12. Explain two benefits of a quota (4)

13. Explain two problems of a quota (4)

14. Explain two other forms of protectionism (4)

15. For each situation which form of protectionism would be most appropriate? (5)
a) A country has slightly higher costs of production than its international rivals

b) A country has many new firms trying to get established in a market

c) A country is having a trade dispute with another country

d) A country has high production standards making its goods more expensive

e) A country is producing goods of slightly lower quality than its competitors

15. What is a trading bloc? (1)

16. Give an example of a trading bloc (1)

17. What is a bilateral agreement? (1)

18. What is a multilateral agreement? (1)

19. What is a free trade area? (2)

20. What is a customs union? (2)

21. What is a common market? (2)

22. What is an economic union? (2)

23. What is a monetary union? (2)

24. Which of the above is the European Union? (1)

25. Which of the above is the Eurozone? (1)

26. Explain how greater integration can lead to greater efficiency (2)

27. Explain how greater integration can lead to greater consumer surplus (2)

28. Explain two benefits of monetary union (4)

29. Explain two costs of monetary union (4)

30. Explain why greater integration could lead to higher unemployment (2)

31. Define trade creation (2)

32. Draw a diagram to illustrate trade creation (4)

33. Use your diagram to identify the following (6)
a) Original level of imports

b) New level of imports

c) Additional trade created

d) Lost tax revenue

e) Original consumer surplus

f) New consumer surplus

34. Define trade diversion (2)

35. Draw a diagram to illustrate trade diversion away from a lower cost producer which is not part of the trading bloc. Country A is the home country; country B is part of the trading bloc; country C is not part of the trading bloc and is the most efficient producer (4)

36. Use your diagram to identify the following (3)
a) level of imports if country C were part of the trading bloc

b) Level of imports from country B when a tariff is imposed on country C

c) Tax revenue lost due to importing from country B rather than country C

37. Explain how trade creation can help achieve WTO objectives (2)

38. Explain how trade diversion conflicts with WTO objectives (2)

Chapter 4 Balance of Payments

1. Define balance of payments (1)

2. What does it mean by balance of payments equilibrium? (1)

3. What does it mean by balance of payments disequilibrium? (1)

4. Does the balance of payments record the value or volume of goods and services? (1)

5. What are the four main sections of the current account? (4)

6. Give two examples of items which can be found on each section of the current account (8)

7. If the value of exports is greater than the value of imports there will be a current account. [ ] (1)

8. If the value of exports is less than the value of imports there will be a current account. [ ] (1)

9. If the value of exports is equal to the value of imports there will be a. [ ] current account (1)

10. The UK usually has a [ ] on its trade in goods and a [ ] on trade in services (2)

11. For each factor state and **explain** which section from the current account the transaction can be found and whether there will be an improvement or worsening of the UK current account (22)

a) Income in the UK increases

b) Incomes abroad increase

c) More people work in the UK and send money home

d) UK citizens who have a holiday home in France rent it out to French citizens

e) The value of the pound increases

f) Inflation in the UK is higher than other countries

g) UK goods improve in quality

h) UK hosts a major sporting event

i) More UK businesses set up in Europe and make profit

j) The EU erects trade barriers against the UK

k) Interest rates in the UK increase

12. Explain two problems with a deficit on the current account (4)

13. Explain two reasons why a deficit might not be a problem (4)

14. Explain two problems with a deficit on the current account (4)

15. Explain two reasons why a surplus is desirable (4)

16. Explain what it means by expenditure switching policies (2)

17. Explain what it means by expenditure reducing policies (2)

18. Explain three policies the government could use to improve a deficit on the current account of the balance of payment (6)

19. Give three examples of items which can be found on the capital/financial account (3)

20. Where would income from the capital account such as interest be recorded? (1)

21. For each situation state whether the current or capital account will be impacted and whether it would be recorded as an import or export on the UK balance of payments (12)
a) A UK citizen buys a holiday home in Germany

b) The holiday home is rented out to German citizens

c) A Japanese citizen moves to the UK and buys a house

d) The work for a Japanese company and send some money home

e) A UK citizen buys shares on the US stock exchange

f) They receive dividends for these shares

Chapter 5 Exchange Rates

1. Define exchange rates (2)

   The value of one currency in terms of another

2. Define nominal exchange rate (1)

3. Define real exchange rate (1)

4. Trade weighted exchange rate (1)

5. What are the two main exchange rate systems? (2)

   - Floating exchange rate
   - Fixed exchange rate

6. What does it mean by a devaluation of the exchange rate? (1)

   A deliberate reduction in currency value to increase export competitiveness

7. What is the difference between a depreciation and devaluation of the exchange rate? (2)

   - Depreciation is a natural decline in value due to market factors
   - Devaluation is an internal reduction in value by the gov

8. What does it mean by appreciation of the exchange rate? (1)

An increase in currency value due to higher market demand

9. What is the difference between appreciation and revaluation? (2)

- Appreciation is a market driven increase in value
- Revaluation is a government led increase in value

10. Give two advantages of a floating exchange rate system (2)

- Automatic adjustment to economic conditions
- Independance in domestic monetary policy

11. Give two disadvantages of a floating exchange rate system (2)

- Volatility and unpredictability
- Vulnerable to speculation

12. Give two advantages of a fixed exchange rate system (2)

- Stability for international trade
- Helps control inflation

13. Give two disadvantages of a fixed exchange rate system (2)

- Limits monetary policy flexibility
- Risk of speculative attacks

14. Draw a diagram to show what will happen to the exchange rate if there is an increase in demand for pounds (2)

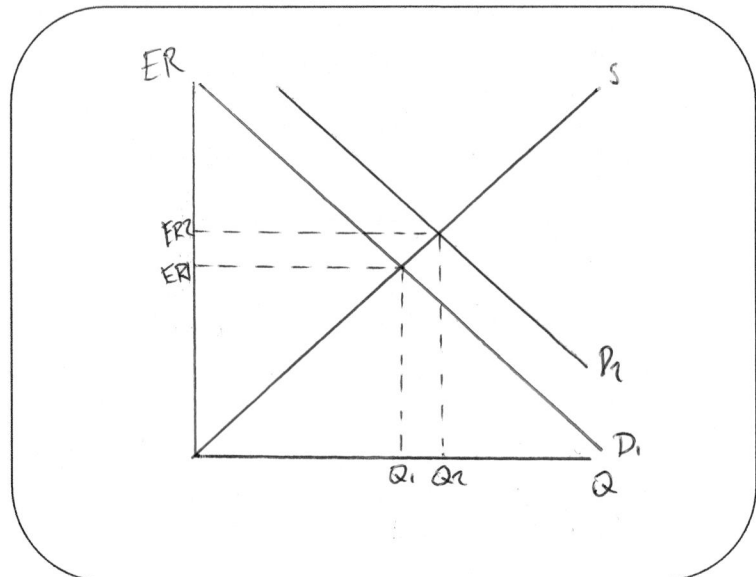

15. Draw a digraph to show what will happen to the exchange rate if there is an increase in supply of pounds (2)

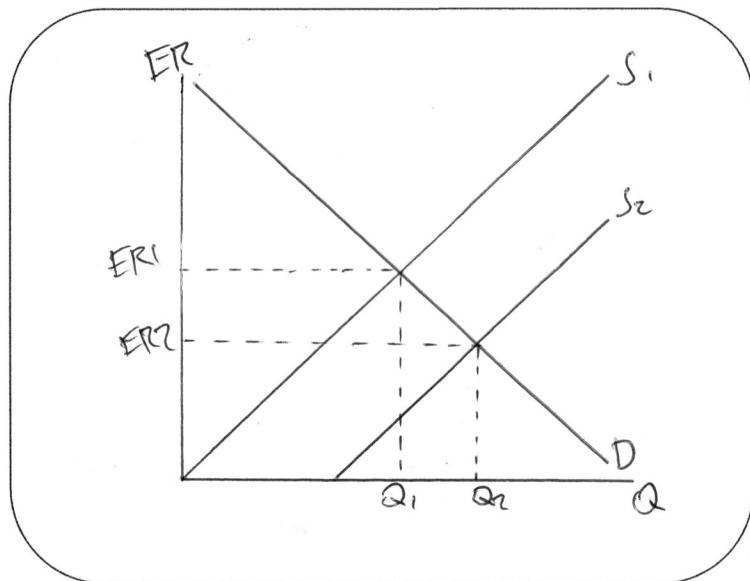

16. For each question which state whether there will be an increase in supply of pounds or an increase in demand for pounds. Explain your answer (22)

a) The quality of UK goods improves

Increase in demand. Higher quality increases foreign purchases of English goods

b) The quality of foreign goods improves

Increase in supply. UK demands more foreign goods

c) Weather in the UK is poor in the summer

Increase in ~~demand~~ supply. UK residents go on holiday and less tourism

d) Inflation in the UK is higher than other countries

Increase in supply. UK goods less competitive

e) Interest rates in the UK increase

Increase in demand. Attracts foreign capital investment

f) Inflation in the UK is lower than in other countries

Increase in demand. UK goods more competitive

g) The UK sells reserves of pounds

Increase in supply. Increases market supply of the pound

h) The UK sells reserves of foreign currency

Increase in demand. Other countries buy the pound with foreign currency, increasing pound demand

i) More foreign workers come into the UK

> Increase in supply. Workers convert earnings to pounds

j) The UK becomes more attractive for FDI

> Increase in demand. Foreign investors buy pounds

k) Speculators expect the value of the pound to increase

> Increase in demand. Foreign investors buy pounds anticipating future

17. The value of the pound increase. What will be the impact on the following
a) Exports — Decrease

b) Imports — Increase

c) Net trade — Worsen

d) Current account of balance of payments — Worsen

e) Aggregate demand — Decrease

f) Economic growth — Slower

g) Inflation   Decrease

h) Unemployment   Rise

17. Explain using a diagram two ways in which the government can intervene to increase the value of a currency (6)

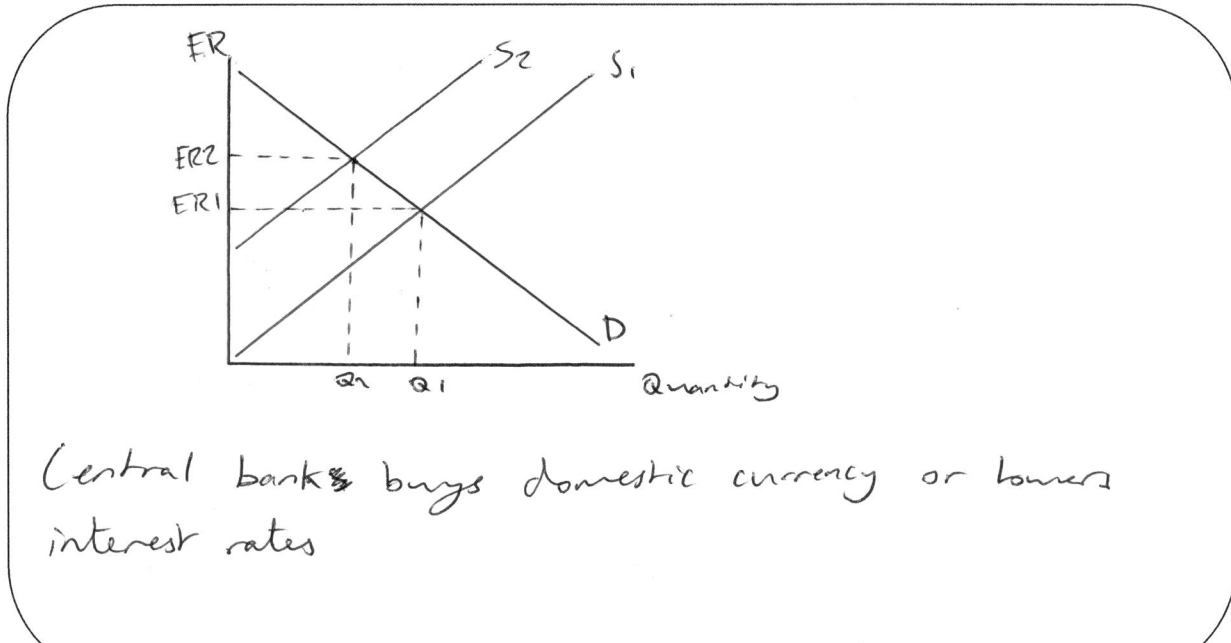

Central bank buys domestic currency or lowers interest rates

18. Explain using a diagram two ways in which the government can intervene to decrease the value of a currency (6)

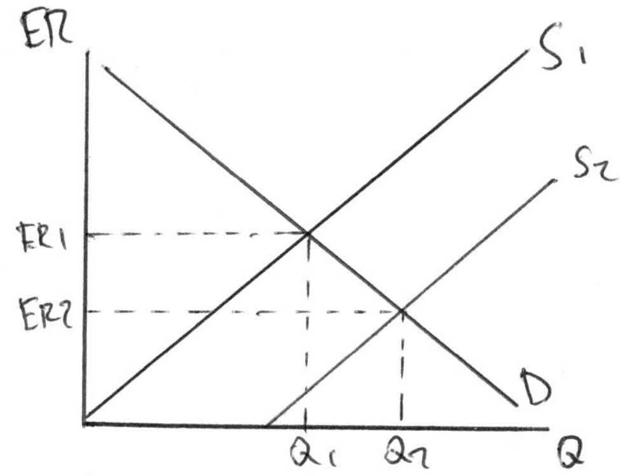

Central bank sells domestic currency or lowers interest rates

19. Draw the J-curve (2)

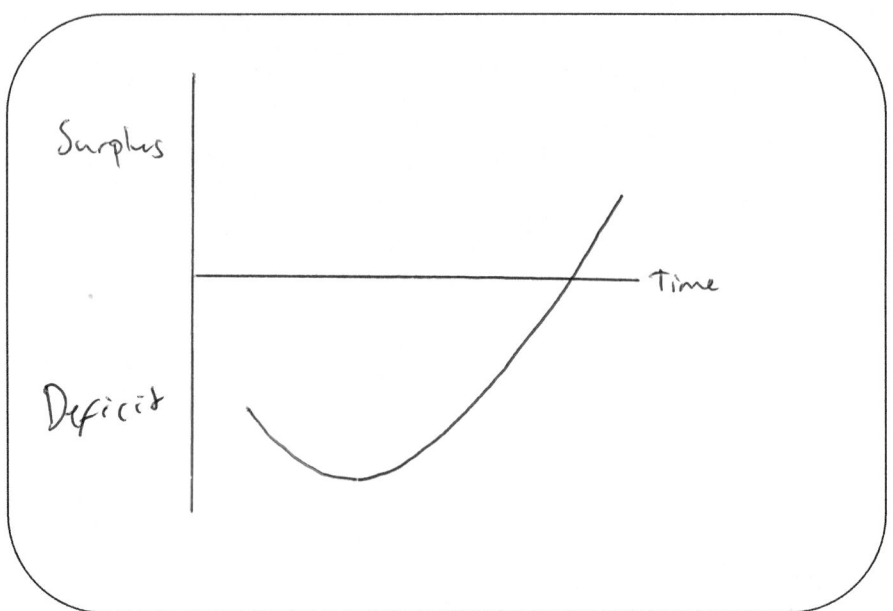

20. Explain what the J curve shows (2)

Illustrates how a countries trade balance initially worsens after devaluation before improving as exports become more competitive

21. What is the Marshall-Lerner condition (2)

?

22. Explain how exchange rates impact a countries competitiveness (2)

Chapter 6 Poverty and Inequality

1. What is a progressive tax? Give an example (2)

2. Explain one problem with a progressive tax (2)

3. What is a means tested benefit? (1)

4. Explain one problem with means tested benefits (2)

5. What is capital gains tax? (1)

6. What is inheritance tax? (1)

7. What is a transfer payment? Give an example (2)

8. Explain how the above taxes improve equality (2)

9. What is the difference between equity and equality? (2)

10. For each statement state whether it is an example of equality, inequality, equity or inequity (4)
a) A doctor earns more than a nurse

b) A part time worker earns less than a full time worker

c) A male and female cleaner earn different amounts

d) A newly qualified teacher earns less than a head of department

11. Give three examples of wealth (3)

12. Explain why having more wealth often leads to more income (2)

13. Draw a diagram of a Lorenz curve (2)

14. What is the formula for calculating the Gini coefficient? (2)

15. What does it mean if the Gini coefficient is 0? (1)

16. What does it mean if the Gini coefficient is 1? (1)

17. What is the poverty trap? (2)

18. Explain why means tested benefits increases the poverty trap (2)

19. Explain three positives of an unequal distribution of income (6)

20. Explain three problems with an unequal distribution of income (6)

21. Define absolute poverty (2)

22. Define relative poverty (2)

23. Give three causes of poverty (3)

24. Give three problems with poverty (3)

25. Give two examples of state provision and explain how they reduce inequality (4)

26. Explain how the NMW will reduce poverty (2)

27. Explain how the NMW might increase poverty (2)

28. Explain how economic growth could reduce poverty (2)

29. Explain how economic growth could increase inequality (2)

Chapter 7 Development

1. Define economic development (2)

2. What does it mean by sustainable development? (2)

3. If there is economic development will there also be economic growth? Explain why (2)

4. If there is economic growth will there also be economic development? Explain why (2)

5. What are the three components which make up the Human Development Index? (3)

6. Explain three problems with using HDI as a measure of development (6)

7. Explain three other indicators which would be a useful measurement of development (6)

8. Explain the meaning of GNI per capita (2)

9. Why is it important to use per capita? (1)

10. Explain three problems with using GNI per capita as a measure of development (6)

11. Explain how investment can promote development (2)

12. Explain the meaning of 'savings gap' (2)

13. What is the Harrod-Domar model? (3)

14. Why does capital flight limit investment? (2)

15. What does it mean by foreign exchange/currency gap? (2)

16. What is bilateral aid? (1)

17. What is multilateral aid? (1)

18. What is tied aid? (1)

19. State three benefits of development aid (3)

21. State three problems with development aid (3)

22. What does is mean by debt relief? (1)

23. Give two problems of debt relief? (2)

24. Explain how fair trade schemes work (2)

25. Explain the meaning of micro finance schemes (2)

26. Why does lack of property rights lead to less investment (2)

27. Explain why low education levels limit development (2)

28. Why does a fast growing population limit development? (2)

29. Give 4 examples of infrastructure required for development (4)

30. Why does poor infrastructure limit FDI? (2)

31. Explain two reasons why dependency on primary products a risk for countries? (4)

32. Why are volatile prices a problem for producers? (2)

33. Why does corruption within a country make it hard to attract FDI? (2)

34. Explain the Lewis model (2)

35. Explain two ways in which the tourism industry can be improved to promote development (4)

36. Give two problems of relying on the tourism industry to promote development (2)

37. What is the meaning of import substitution? (1)

38. Explain why a floating exchange rate helps a market react to international demand (2)

39. How could FDI be promoted? (1)

40. Explain how protectionism can increase economic growth (2)

Edexcel and OCR

41. What is the purpose of the IMF? (2)

42. What is the purpose of the World Bank? (2)

43. What are NGOs and what do they do? (2)

Chapter 8 The Financial Sector

1. Give 4 functions of money (4)

2. Give 4 characteristics of money (4)

3. Give 3 different forms of borrowing (3)

4. What is the difference between debt finance and equity finance? (2)

5. Explain how the financial sector aids economic growth (2)

6. Explain what is meant by the forwards market for currency (2)

7. Why do firms buy on the forwards market? (2)

8. Give an example of a commercial bank (1)

9. What is the difference between a commercial bank and an investment bank? (2)

10. State whether each of the following is a role of a commercial bank or investment bank (7)
a) Lend to firms

b) Lend to individuals

c) Arrange share and bond issues

d) Provide insurance to individuals

e) Buy and sell securities

f) Offer advise on mergers and acquisitions

g) Offer mortgages

<u>Q11- 13 AQA only</u>

11. What are the two main sections on the commercial banks balance sheet? (2)

12. What are the three objectives of a commercial bank? (3)

13. Using an example, explain how achieving one of these objectives could make another one worse (2)

14. What is the meaning of the inter-bank lending rate? (1)

15. Explain how banks create credit (2)

16. What is the difference between narrow and broad money? (2)

Q17- 18 AQA and Edexcel

17. What is the meaning of moral hazard? (2)

18. Give an example of moral hazard in financial markets (2)

Q19- 25 Edexcel only

19. Using an example of the financial crisis, explain why externalities exist in financial markets (3)

20. What is the meaning of asymmetric information? (2)

21. Give an example of asymmetric information in financial markets (2)

22. Explain the meaning of market rigging (2)

23. Give an example of how this might happen in financial markets (2)

24. Explain how an individual could make money by speculating on the currency market (2)

25. Explain how excessive speculation can lead to market bubbles (2)

26. What is the name of the central bank in the UK? (1)

27. Give two reasons why the central bank need to act as lender of last resort (2)

28. Give two problems of acting as lender of last resort (2)

29. What is the other main role of the central bank? (1)

30. What is the meaning of capital ratio? (2)

31. What is the meaning of liquidity ratio? (2)

32. Why did the rules on the above ratios need to be tightened after the financial crisis? (2)

33. Explain how these restrictions could restrict economic growth (2)

34. Explain the role of the FPC in regulating financial markets (2)

35. Explain the role of the PRA in regulating financial markets (2)

36. Explain the role of the FCA in regulating financial markets (2)

37. Which two organisations regulate the global financial system? (2)

Chapter 9 Government Intervention

1. Define fiscal policy (2)

2. Define and give an example of a progressive tax (2)

3. Define and give an example of a regressive tax (2)

4. Define and give an example of a proportional tax (2)

5. Explain which type of tax should be used to reduce inequality (2)

6. Explain the link between a regressive tax and the trickle down effect (2)

7. Draw a Laffer curve (2)

8. Explain what the Laffer curve shows (2)

9. Define and give an example of current government spending (2)

10. Define and give an example of capital government spending (2)

11. Define and give an example of transfer payments (2)

12. Explain what happens to government spending and taxation in a recession (4)

13. Explain what happens to government spending and taxation when economic growth is high (4)

14. Explain the meaning of a cyclical deficit (2)

15. Explain the meaning of a structural deficit (2)

16. What is the difference between a budget deficit and national debt? (2)

17. Explain two reasons why a budget deficit is a problem (4)

18. Explain two circumstances under which a budget deficit is not a problem (4)

19. The government could increase direct tax to reduce a budget deficit. What will be the impact on the following (5)
a) Incentives to work

b) Income distribution

c) Real output

d) Employment

e) Profit

f) Price level

g) Investment

20. Why does the government have fiscal rules? (2)

21. Explain the role of the OBR (2)

22. Other than during a recession, state two reasons why government spending might increase (2)

23. What will be the impact on the following of an increase in government spending as a proportion of GDP (5)
a) Living standards

b) Equality

c) Productivity

d) Economic growth

e) Price level

24. Explain, using the concept of crowding out how an increase in government spending could reduce private sector investment. Use an example to help. (4)

25. Define monetary policy (2)

26. Explain how an increase in the interest rate will lead to an increase in the exchange rate (3)

27. Explain how a depreciation of the exchange rate will lead to an increase in competitiveness (3)

28. Explain how quantitative easing leads to an increase in the money supply (2)

30. Give two reasons why QE might not lead to an increase in consumption (2)

30. Fill in the gaps to explain the transmission mechanism when there is a reduction in the official base rate (10)
a) interest rates on savings and mortgages

b) House prices will likely

c) Consumer confidence

d) Consumption

e) Exchange rates

f) Demand for exports

g) Demand for imports

h) Net trade

i) Overall AD

j) Inflation

31. Explain the meaning of the natural rate or unemployment (2)

32. Draw a diagram of the Phillips curve (2)

33. If the government wants to reduce unemployment what does the Phillips curve suggest they should do? (1)

34. Explain why inflation expectations can lead to further inflation (2)

35. Explain why wage increases could lead to unemployment (2)

36. Use your answers to the previous two questions to help explain, using a diagram the concept of shifting the short run Phillips curve and the existence of the long run Phillips curve (8)

37. The Phillips curve suggests low employment and low inflation cannot exist together. Explain using a diagram, why supply curve polices can allow both objectives to be achieved (6)

38. Explain how a cut in income tax leads to an increase in aggregate supply (2)

39. Explain how privatisation influences the supply side of the economy (2)

40. Explain how reducing unemployment benefits influences the supply side of the economy (2)

41. Explain how trade union reform influences the supply side of the economy (2)

42. Explain how spending on education and training influences the supply side of the economy (2)

43. Give an example of an unintended consequence of one supply side policy measure (1)

44. Draw a diagram to show how supply side policies can achieve lower inflation and lower unemployment (3)

45. Pick four different supply side policies and state one problem of each (4)

46. State and explain two supply side policies which will also have an impact on AD (4)

47. Explain two reasons why the desired outcome might not be achieved when implementing any policies (4)

Self-Evaluation

	I understand this well	I struggled with some of this	This was really difficult so needs more work
Chapter 1			
Chapter 2			
Chapter 3			
Chapter 4			
Chapter 5			
Chapter 6			
Chapter 7			
Chapter 8			
Chapter 9			

Additional Notes

Additional Notes

Additional Notes

Additional Notes

Additional Notes

Additional Notes

Printed in Great Britain
by Amazon